Buddy'
New Friend

by **P.T. Finch**

Illustrated by Gokhan Bas

Published in the United States by Literary Mango, Inc.

Little Neck, New York. First edition, 2017.

www.literarymango.com

Discounts are available on quantity purchases by corporations, associations and others. For details, contact us through the website above.

Author: P.T. Finch

Illustrator: Gokhan Bas

Editor: Jody Mullen

Summary: Toddlers Luna and Asher are away at school, and their pet cat Buddy gets lonely. To solve this problem, the family decides to go to the local animal shelter and adopt a dog.

Paperback ISBN 978-1-946844-09-5

Hardcover ISBN 978-1-946844-10-1

It was too rainy to play outdoors. Luna and Asher had been building block towers all morning.

"I'm tired of castles," said Asher.
"Let's build something different."

"How about a block house for
Buddy?" asked Luna.

"That sounds like a good idea!" Asher agreed. "Buddy! Hey, Buddy!" he called.

Buddy, the family's cat, wandered in, as gloomy as the rain. "Hey Buddy, let's play!" said Luna.

But Buddy didn't look like he wanted to play. "What's wrong, kitty cat?" she asked.

Just then, Daddy came in.

"Daddy, what's the matter
with Buddy?" Asher asked.
"He's not happy."

Daddy knelt down and petted Buddy.
"What's the matter, big guy?" he asked.

Luna wished Buddy could tell her.

"Is Buddy sick?" worried Asher.

"I don't think so," said Daddy. "Can you think of another reason he might be feeling blue?"

"I don't know," Luna admitted.
"I don't want him to be sad."

"Maybe he's lonely when we aren't home," said Asher.

"I have an idea," said Daddy. "How would you two
like to find a friend for Buddy? Mommy and I think
it would be nice for us to have our very own dog."

'Yes! I've always wanted a dog!" cried Asher.
'Can we go to the pet store?"

"Well, the pet store is one place to get a dog," said Daddy. "But we think it would be nice to visit an animal shelter."

"Animal shelter?" asked Luna. "What's that?"

"An animal shelter is a home for dogs and cats who don't have a family," Mommy explained as she came into the room. "Would you like to find a dog who needs a home?"

"Yes!" said Asher. "We can give a dog a good home!"

That afternoon, Daddy, Mommy, Luna, and Asher visited the shelter. Other families were there to adopt a pet, too. Luna and Asher and the other children loved meeting all the puppies. Then, Asher noticed a scruffy older dog watching them.

"Daddy, that dog looks like he needs a friend!" said Asher. Luna held her hand up to the dog's soft muzzle, and he licked her fingers as if to say, *I do need a friend.*

"This dog loves kids," said a volunteer. "He used to belong to a wonderful family. But they moved to another country and couldn't take him. His name is Sam. He's so sweet and quiet. We never even hear him bark."

"But this dog should live in a nice house and play with kids!" said Luna. "Mommy, Daddy, can we please take Sam home?"
"Yes, please?" agreed Asher.

Mommy and Daddy smiled at each other. "I think it would be nice to give this dog a home," said Mommy. "And I think it's *very* nice that you two noticed him."

The family brought Sam home that very day, just as the sun was coming out. Luna was excited for him to meet Buddy!

But when Buddy came around a corner
and saw a big dog, he turned and raced
out of the room. He was afraid of Sam!

Mommy explained that it might take a few days for Buddy and Sam to get used to each other. She said they might have to be patient.

ON SUNDAY

Sam tried to eat Buddy's food.
Buddy was not happy!

ON MONDAY

Sam tried to sleep in Buddy's bed.
Buddy didn't like that much, either.

ON TUESDAY

Sam stepped on Buddy's tail.
Buddy really didn't like that!

uddy wouldn't leave the bathroom. He only
ame out when Sam was out for a walk.

That night, Luna
couldn't eat her dinner.
"What's the matter,
Luna?" Mommy asked.
Luna began to cry.

"Buddy and Sam aren't friends!" said Luna. "I'm afraid you're going to make us give Sam back to the shelter!"

"Let's try something," said Daddy. He slipped a leash around Sam's neck and said, "Sit, Sam. Stay." Then he retrieved Buddy from the bathroom. Buddy's eyes grew wide when he saw Sam, but Daddy held him safely.

Buddy watched Sam carefully. When he saw that Sam was just sitting quietly, he grew curious. He hopped off Daddy's lap and crept up to Sam. He sniffed Sam, and Sam waited patiently.

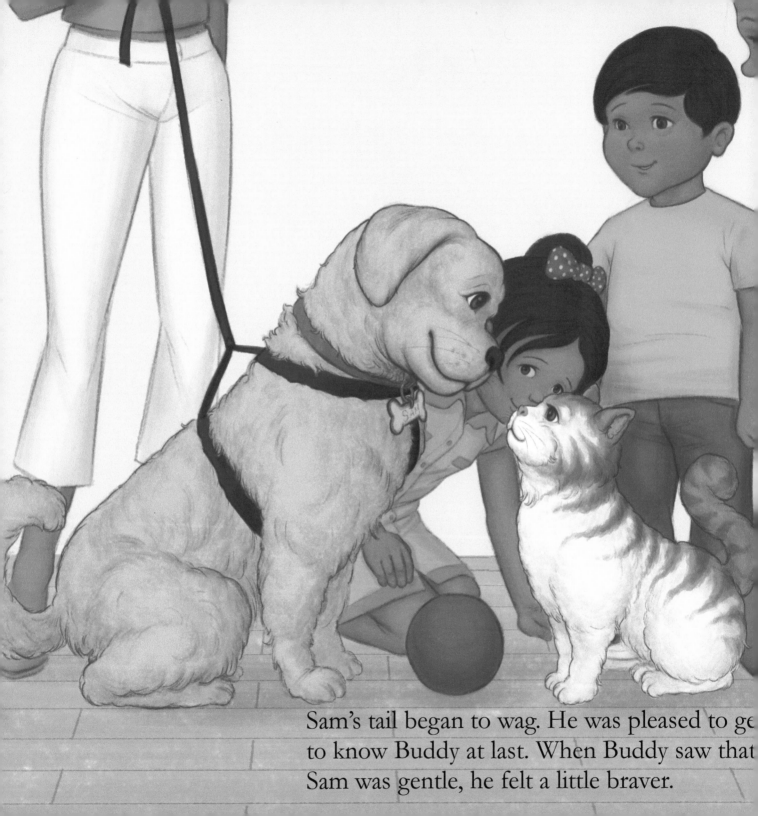

Sam's tail began to wag. He was pleased to get to know Buddy at last. When Buddy saw that Sam was gentle, he felt a little braver.

"Look at that!" cried Asher. "I think they like each other!"

"See?" said Mommy. "Sometimes you just have to be patient."

After dinner, Asher drew a picture of Buddy and Sam, and Luna colored it in. "We'll hang this one in the hall," said Daddy. "That way, Sam can remember the day he found a new family. Right, Sam?"

And for the first time since they'd brought him home, Sam gave a big, happy bark

DISCUSSION QUESTIONS

Why do you think Buddy was sad in the beginning of the story?

Why did the family choose to adopt a pet at the animal shelter instead of buying one from the pet store?

Why did Asher choose Sam, the scruffy older dog, over all of the cute puppies at the shelter?

What are some possible reasons behind animals staying in the shelter?

Why do you think Buddy was scared of Sam?

How did the family help Buddy overcome his fear of Sam?

Try These Children's Books

Animals Can Sing by MO Lufkin is a fun story where the reader goes on a short adventure in the woods. You'll visit with the bees, a wolf pup and other animals as you go deeper into a mystical forest. Told in rhyme, this delightful and fun children's picture book comes to life with a musical score that you can sing to, while enjoying the beautiful landscape illustrations of natural scenery that enhance your literary journey and captivate the imaginations of young readers.

Thinking of Mom by MO Lufkin is a heartfelt story about loss. Mom takes care of Ella every day. But when Mom is overcome with illness, Ella is left feeling sad, angry, and helpless and doesn't know how to deal with those emotions. Dad helps Ella to call on the good memories of Mom to help her feel happy again. Children coping with loss and the grown-ups who love them will find comfort in this engaging and empathetic story told alongside beautiful watercolor images.

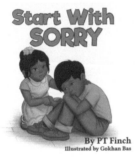

In *Start With Sorry* by PT Finch, Three-year-old Luna loves to spend time with her older brother, Asher, and she wants to do everything he does. But when they sit down to draw pictures together, Luna feels upset that she can't do everything he can do. When she reacts in anger, Asher is sad and doesn't want to color with her anymore. With Mommy's help, Luna learns how to make amends for hurting her brother's feelings. Kids love this story, and adults appreciate the valuable lesson it teaches about empathy for others.

www.literarymango.com

Literary Mango

CPSIA information can be obtained
at www.ICGtesting.com
Printed in the USA
BVHW020139120520
579551BV00002B/9